Adventures In Eating With The Nutrition Champion Of Kids

"Adventures in eating will now begin.
Come along with me, read this book I'm in.

Nutrition Champion of Kids, that's me.
Listening to what I say is the key.

Meet my food friends in the Food Pyramid.
Learn to eat healthy and smart as a kid.

To be sure you have fun, here's my one clue . . .
Never be afraid to try something new!"

Pyramid Pal

Come let us all learn the **FOOD PYRAMID**.
Eating should always be fun for a kid!

Most important for you to do each day,
Eat healthy food, second only to play.

See the **PYRAMID** rise tall in the air.
Learn all the lessons that it will now share.

Eating from the five food groups every day,
Keeps you healthy, it's the very best way.

More foods from the bottom, less from the top,
Eating right can be fun, read on, don't stop…

Since there's no one right food that you should eat,
Come with us, the food groups you will now meet.

The **PYRAMID** base, it's big and it's strong.
You'll find the **GRAIN** GROUP, eat lots all day long.

VEGETABLES and **FRUITS** are delicious treats.
Topping the **GRAIN** GROUP, they have preferred seats.

High on the **PYRAMID**, who does belong?
The **MILK** and **MEAT** GROUPS are tagging along.

The top, tiny GROUP, don't eat to excess.
For **FATS**, **OILS** and **SWEETS**, it's best to have less.

What are the right foods you should daily munch,
What choices for breakfast, dinner and lunch?

These are good questions, and you will soon know,
What you should eat to be smart, run and grow.

Your energy comes from foods that you eat.
So, healthy meals daily are hard to beat.

Eat from each group for a healthy diet.
When you read these books, you'll want to try it.

Open your mind, sing out in a loud voice,
"The rest of my life good foods are my choice!"

"Adventures in eating will now begin.
Come along with me, read this book I'm in.

Nutrition Champion of Kids, that's me.
Listening to what I say is the key.

Meet my food friends in the Food Pyramid.
Learn to eat healthy and smart as a kid.

To be sure you have fun, here's my one clue . . .
Never be afraid to try something new!"

Pyramid Pal

Eat from the **GRAIN** GROUP, that is good advice.
Munch down Bread, Cereal, Pasta and Rice.

These four foods are a main energy source.
It is one group healthy eaters endorse.

These **GRAINS** hold up all the other group parts.
At the bottom is where good eating starts.

Here come the Breads, each has a special tale.
Enjoy their stories before they go stale.

Molly **Muffin** danced into the breadbox.
Bernie **Bagel,** he snuck in like a fox.

Out of the toaster, Wilma **Waffle** shot.
Pierre **Pretzel** watched, all tied in a knot.

Holly **Hot Dog Bun** searched for Frank Furter.
Then begged yellow Meg Mustard to squirt her.

Hector **Hamburger Bun** crawled from his bag.
Since he was whole wheat, he wanted to brag.

Whitney **White Bread** dropped in from out of town.
Patricia **Pancake** flip-flopped like a clown.

Todd **Tortilla** came rolled tight as can be,
While Caroline **Cracker** screamed, "Don't Crunch Me!"

Next for all families, here's a food "must",
Some lip smacking things piled on **Pizza Crust**.

Not to be left out of the **GRAIN** GROUP fun,
Cereals parade, marching one by one.

George **Granola** dove right into the bowl.
Carlos **Corn Flakes** climbed up out of his hole.

Pam **Puffed Rice** almost exploded with glee.
"I'm thrilled to have all my friends here with me."

Bob **Bran Flakes** screamed, "In milk, they are drowning."
So in he splashed, but found they were clowning.

Oscar **Oatmeal** bubbled up with delight.
Strawberry topped, he was feeling just right.

Now, for Pasta, you will have to admit,
In hot water, it cooks lickity split.

Benny **Bow Tie** plunged down into the pot,
Followed by Susie **Shell**, sailing her yacht.

Lance **Lasagna** sang opera, watch him jump.
Ralph **Ravioli,** stuffed with cheese, was plump.

Sylvester **Spaghetti** tripped, slipped and slid,
Proud to be part of the **FOOD PYRAMID**.

Nicky **Noodles** felt like a stringy fool,
But leaped right on in after Pasta school.

Polly **Pop Corn,** once a kernel, then "pop".
She sure changed her look when she popped her top.

Very important, not to be left out,
Is the Rice family, all wanting to shout.

"When a fine meal, you're trying to create,
With meat, fish, chicken, Rice always tastes great."

Wendy **White Rice** sloshed into hot water.
It felt so great, she then called her daughter.

Billy **Brown Rice** spied them having such fun.
He said, "I'll join you till we are all done."

This main source of energy, **GRAINS** are best.
They score big on the Carbohydrate test.

Carbohydrates help you play all day long.
They give you a boost and help you stay strong.

A lot of Fiber can also be found
In all of these **GRAINS** that come from the ground.

Fiber's main job is to move food through you,
Making your insides feel sparkling and new.

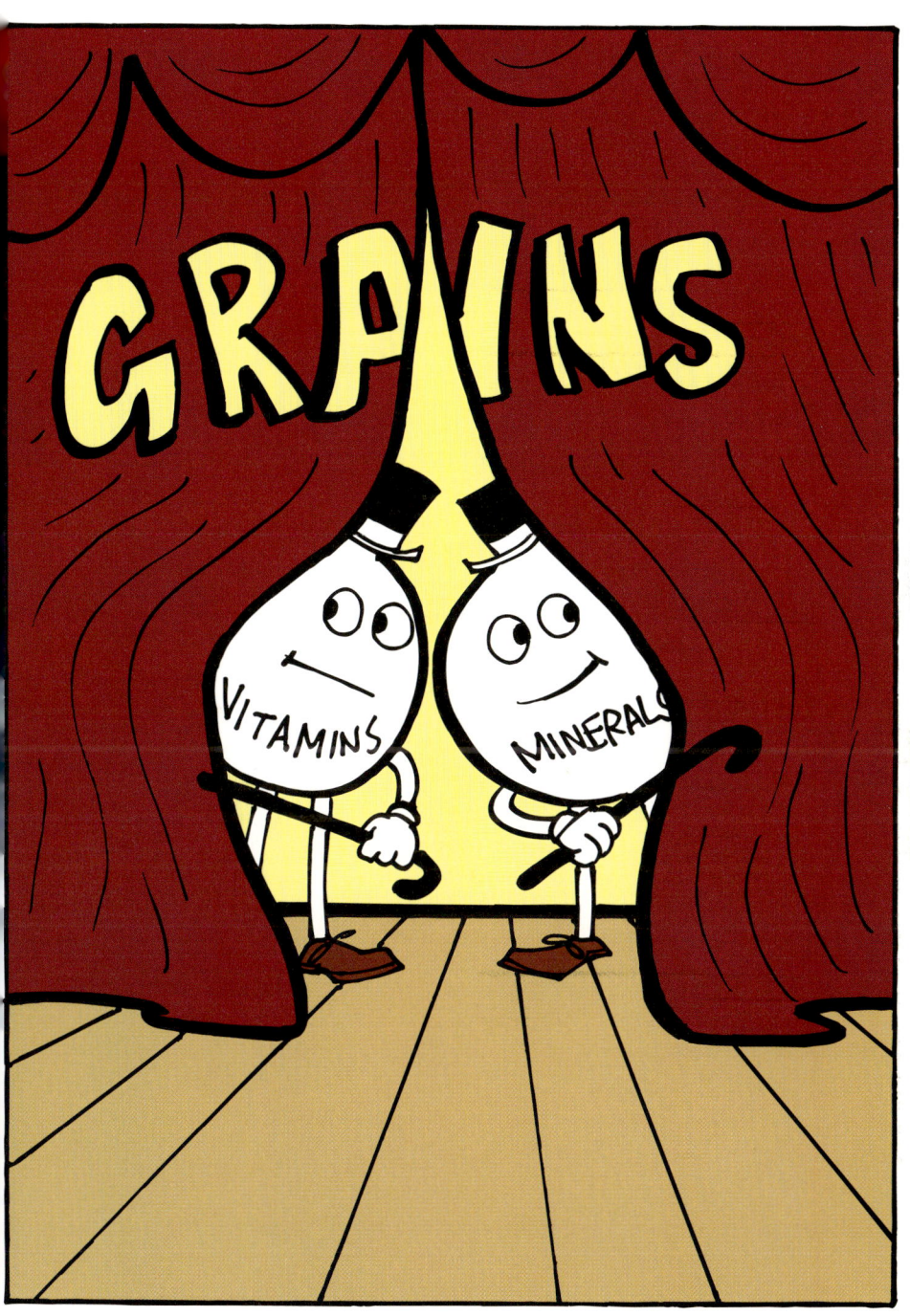

In **GRAINS**, Vitamins and Minerals dwell,
Working so hard to build each red blood cell.

Nibble on these breakfast, dinner and lunch.
Six to **eleven** servings daily munch.

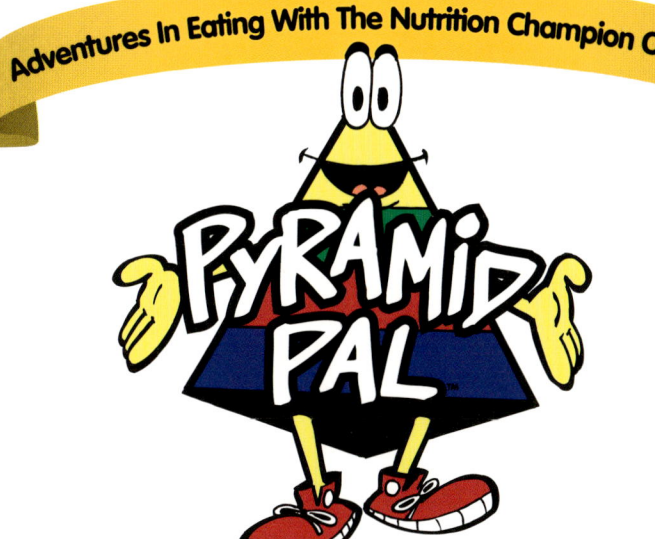

"Adventures in eating will now begin.
Come along with me, read this book I'm in.

Nutrition Champion of Kids, that's me.
Listening to what I say is the key.

Meet my food friends in the Food Pyramid.
Learn to eat healthy and smart as a kid.

To be sure you have fun, here's my one clue . . .
Never be afraid to try something new!"

Pyramid Pal

"Eat your **VEGETABLES**, they are good for you."
These words you have heard since you were brand new.

All sizes and shapes, for eating that's right,
Whether raw or cooked, they're a pure delight.

They're easy to learn, follow this story,
A tale of soup and **VEGETABLE** glory...

Ashley **Asparagus** plunged, eyes closed tight.
Craig **Carrot** waited 'cause he was polite.

Stevie **Spinach** slipped, and then in he fell,
Yanked Zach **Zucchini**, who gave a loud yell.

Brent **Broccoli** spied them swimming around,
Called all the **VEGETABLES** that could be found.

Carl **Corn** flew in on his propeller plane,
Speeding right along to escape the rain.

Gracie **Green Bean** caught a ride with Carl **Corn**,
Grateful for the thrill of being airborne.

Paul **Potato** struggled in through the storm.
Soon to be out of the cold, safe and warm.

Tony **Tomato** jumped into the pot,
Making a big splash before he could rot.

Lucy **Lettuce** spread her green leaves out wide,
Screaming, "All you **Veggies** move to the side!"

Ced **Celery** was mad, so he stalked in.
Claire **Cabbage** leafed through this book with a grin.

Perhaps, you wonder what's good in this soup?
Vitamins, Minerals swirl in each scoop.

They improve eyesight, building blocks are they,
Heal cuts and bruises you get when you play.

Also, Carbohydrates, they sing along,
Proud of their energy boosting soup song.

Then friendly Fiber slides down into you,
Keeping your insides clean and healthy, too.

Very little Fat, Calories are low.
All **VEGETABLES** help keep you on the go.

Needing them daily should be understood.
Three to **five** servings of **VEGGIES** are good.

"Adventures in eating will now begin.
Come along with me, read this book I'm in.

Nutrition Champion of Kids, that's me.
Listening to what I say is the key.

Meet my food friends in the Food Pyramid.
Learn to eat healthy and smart as a kid.

To be sure you have fun, here's my one clue . . .
Never be afraid to try something new!"

Pyramid Pal

"Come learn about **FRUITS**," teachers often say.
"An apple a day keeps doctors away."

Considered to be Mother Nature's gift,
FRUIT each day gives you an energy lift.

All through the year, in good or bad weather,
Eat them alone or all tossed together.

The **FRUIT** salad treats that follow this rhyme
Will help you tip toe, run fast, hop and climb.

Paula **Pineapple** leaped into the dish.
Scott **Strawberry** skipped, landing with a squish.

Carrie **Cantaloupe** waddled slowly in.
Ryan **Raisin** ran from where he had been.

Luis **Lemon,** he dawdled, then he jumped.
Into the others, Ben **Banana** bumped.

Barb **Blueberry** floated down on a kite.
Kent **Kiwi** carefully guided her flight.

Wally **Watermelon** rolled off the vine.
Peter **Peach** tumbled in fuzzy and fine.

Annabelle **Apple** plopped down from her tree.
Penelope **Pear** vaulted in with glee.

Gregory Green **Grape** tore off from his bunch,
Asking Olivia **Orange** to have lunch.

Famous for Carbohydrates, good to eat,
FRUIT gives you energy, and can't be beat.

Vitamins A, B and C, so worthwhile,
Help eyes, skin and blood stay in tip-top style.

FRUIT is low in Fat, full of Fiber, too,
Keeps you feeling good in all that you do.

When it comes to **FRUIT**, we just want to say,
Two to **four** servings are perfect each day.

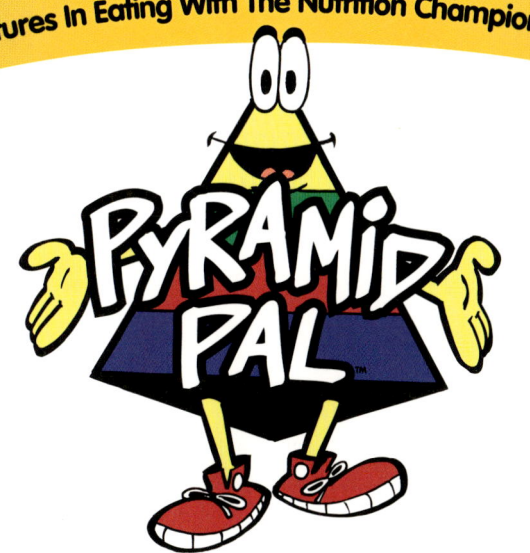

"Adventures in eating will now begin.
Come along with me, read this book I'm in.

Nutrition Champion of Kids, that's me.
Listening to what I say is the key.

Meet my food friends in the Food Pyramid.
Learn to eat healthy and smart as a kid.

To be sure you have fun, here's my one clue . . .
Never be afraid to try something new!"

Pyramid Pal

MILK products include Milk, Yogurt and Cheese, Cold Ice Cream and Frozen Yogurts that please.

Each of these foods is good tasting indeed.
Just a little is what all bodies need.

Margarita **Milk**, she peeked out the door
Of her cool home, the refrigerator.

Slipping and sliding down throats, slick as silk,
Nothing tastes better with cookies than **Milk**.

She poured into a glass, wanting to make
A splashy entrance as a thick **Milkshake**.

Yolanda **Yogurt**, making tongues tingle,
Danced right on in, while singing this jingle...

"I come in fruit flavors. I'm great when cold.
I skate down throats, I am tart, I am bold."

Simon **String Cheese** said, "I'm a food that's fun.
With your fingers peel my strings, one by one.

When you're on the go, whatever you do,
Don't forget to take me along with you."

Say "**Cheese**", with a great big smile, you are told.
Some are mild in taste, some are very bold.

Corinne **Cottage Cheese** laughed with a big grin,
Glad she was low Fat and soon to be thin.

Mike **Mozzarella** screamed, "I'm low Fat, too!"
Onto the top of a pizza, he flew.

Some **Cheeses** are slices, some chunks, some flakes.
Paul **Parmesan**, over pasta he shakes.

Shelby **Swiss** peeked through the holes in her side.
Being a shy **Cheese**, she wanted to hide.

Jonathan **Jack,** a fine flavored fellow,
Said, "I'm easy to love and quite mellow."

Amy **American Cheese** fell on bread.
"When hot, I'm a grilled **Cheese** sandwich," she said.

Fran **Frozen Yogurt** squirts from a machine,
Twirls herself into a new dance routine.

Irving **Ice Cream** plopped from a metal scoop.
All he wanted was to "melt" with the group.

Be sure to eat low Fat food from this group,
'Cause Fat and Calories come in each scoop.

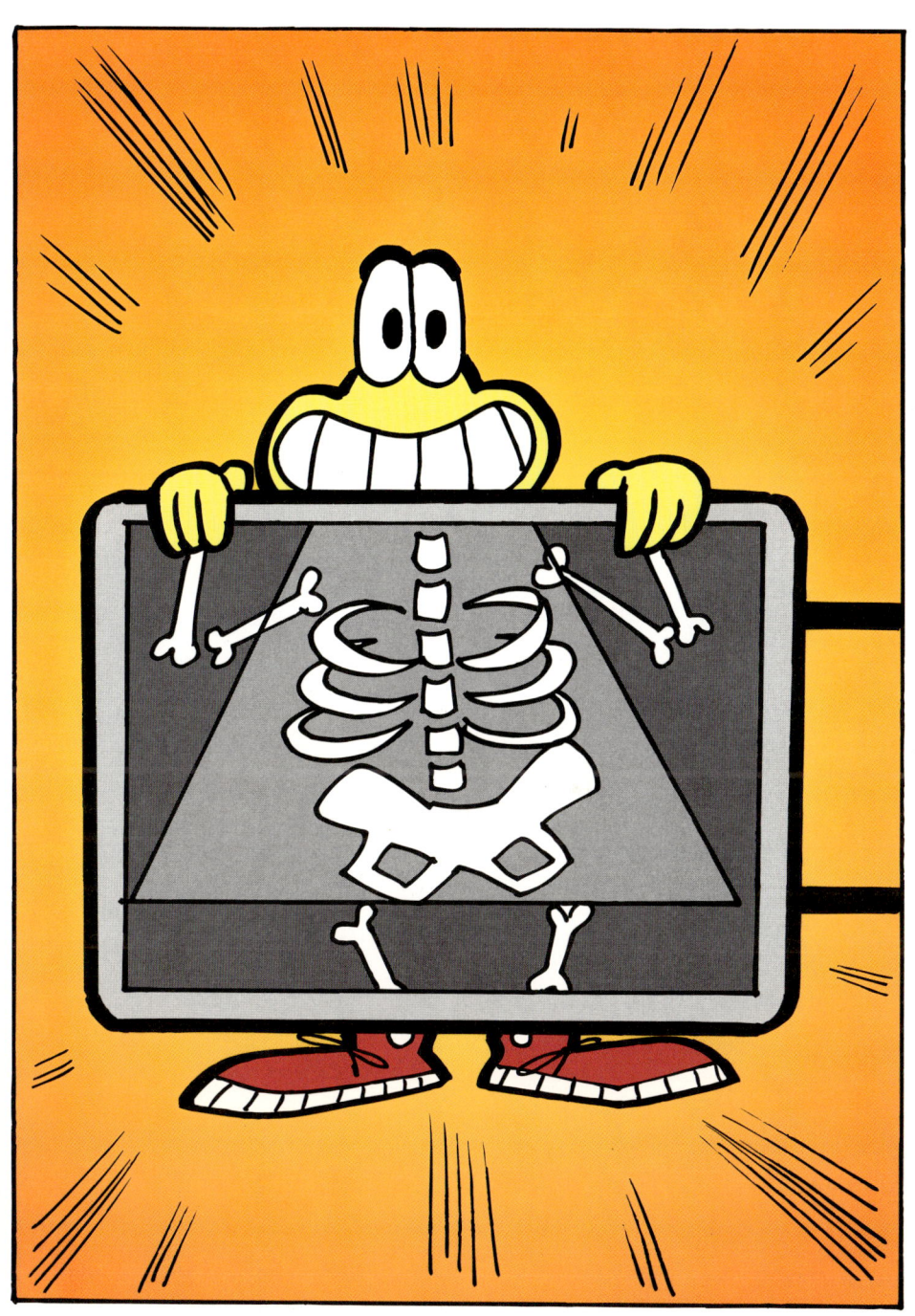

Calcium, Protein and Vitamins, too,
Help build strong bones and teeth to strengthen you.

Everyone finds it easy to agree,
Each day **MILK** servings should be **two** to **three**.

Adventures In Eating With The Nutrition Champion Of Kids

"Adventures in eating will now begin.
Come along with me, read this book I'm in.

Nutrition Champion of Kids, that's me.
Listening to what I say is the key.

Meet my food friends in the Food Pyramid.
Learn to eat healthy and smart as a kid.

To be sure you have fun, here's my one clue . . .
Never be afraid to try something new!"

Pyramid Pal

High on the **PYRAMID**, the **MEAT** GROUP sits,
Important to eat, but in little bits.

It's Meat, Poultry, Nuts, Dry Beans, Eggs and Fish.
To join your diet is their fondest wish.

This GROUP is versatile, they do stand tall,
Being the most complete Proteins of all.

One little problem, a simple fact that,
Many of these foods have a lot of Fat.

Keep right on reading, and you will soon see,
Each has a special personality.

Some graze on the land, some swim in the sea,
Some fly through the air, some grow on a tree.

Harley **Hamburger** from the counter flew,
Wanting to be grilled on the barbecue.

Miss Buffy **Bacon** sizzled as she fried.
"Watch out, I am loaded with Fat," she cried.

Parker **Pork Chop** laughed and opened the door,
Strolling out of the refrigerator.

Luke **Lunch Meats** snuggled into his soft bed.
He felt quite cozy, surrounded by bread.

Ronnie **Roast Beef,** one handsome hunk of Meat,
With his friend, Herb **Ham,** were yummy to eat.

Sebastian **Steak**, out of the broiler flew.
"I will join Harley on the barbecue."

Maria **Meatball** bounced, looking to top
Mounds of spaghetti, that's where she did plop.

Next comes Poultry, in all kinds of weather,
Birds of a feather, they flock together.

Tom **Turkey** roasted in his special pan,
Calling and waving to his **Duck** friend, Dan.

Then Dan **Duck**, excited to join the rest,
Paddled away from his parent's **Duck** nest.

Cynthia **Chicken**, counting one, two, three,
Flapped her fowl feathers and strutted with glee.

Knowing which came first, the **Chicken** or **Egg**,
Is a question, for the answer we beg.

Here comes Ellie the **Egg** with her shell dyed.
She can be scrambled, poached, hard-boiled or fried.

Not to be left out, slip sliding on in,
Come the Fish swimming from where they have been.

Tiffany **Tuna,** she wobbles and sways,
Carefully trying to surf in for days.

Sasha **Salmon** telephoned other Fish,
Telling them how great they'd look on a dish.

Timothy **Trout** glided down through the air,
Soon to be landing, he didn't care where.

Samantha **Shrimp**, dancing in her toutou,
Did a great "Hip Hop" into a Fish stew.

Then Scotty **Swordfish,** a swashbuckling fool,
Joined his Fish friends after sword fighting school.

Christopher **Cod** just splish splashing along,
Belly-flopped from a wave, singing this song.

"I have friends from the sea, friends from the lake.
Cook them with lemon, a great meal they'll make."

Sometimes called Legumes, sometimes called Dry Beans,
Now, you'll find out what this all really means.

Willie **White Bean** sank down into the pot,
Fanning his face, said, "This Jacuzzi's hot!"

Brandy **Black Bean** shouted out as she ran.
"To be the Belle of the Ball is my plan."

Pete **Pinto Bean** galloped fast past the rest
To get the slot in the pot that was best.

Nick **Navy Bean,** with a nautical shout,
Said, "Where are we sailing? Let's come about!"

Stuart **Split Pea** squeezed on out of his pod,
Saying, "This rush to the pot is sure odd".

Pearl **Peanut**, firmly stood still on a knife.
Peanut Butter was her main goal in life.

Seth **Soy Bean**, knowing he would pass the test,
Wanted the others to see he was best.

In rolled a group of Nuts, one, two, three, four,
Happy little Nuts, spinning on the floor.

Clifford **Cashew** stepped into a Nut dish.
To be your favorite Nut was his wish.

Art **Almond**, dressed like a tropical Nut,
Swang in his hammock, outside his Nut hut.

Weston **Walnut**, plain or roasted, was good,
Crowned himself king of his Nut neighborhood.

Phil **Pistachio** bulged out of his shell.
From weight lifting, he saw his muscles swell.

Sunflower Seed Sam, a salty old man,
Joined Clyde **Chestnut** in a hot roasting pan.

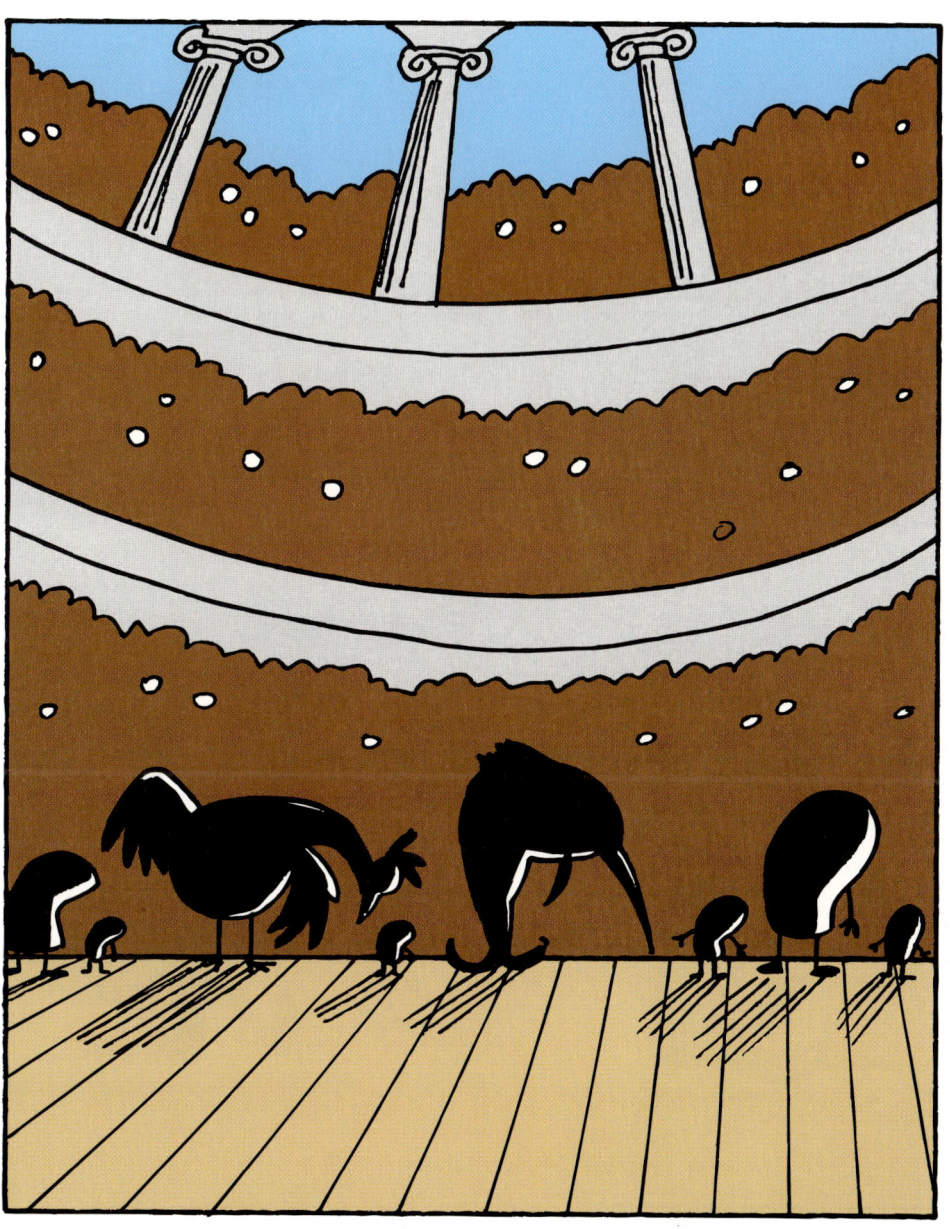

All stars in this GROUP, they each take a bow.
Why they're important, we will tell you now.

You must eat from the **MEAT** GROUP every day.
Put them on your team, it's the winning way.

Your body can't store Protein, it is so.
Yet, still it is key to helping you grow.

It builds tissue, muscle, organs and cells,
Helps fight infections, goes where a germ dwells.

Rich in Iron, these foods do their job well,
Taking Oxygen to each little cell.

Zinc, an important Mineral to know,
Works to protect and help your body grow.

Small portions from this GROUP, you can't go wrong,
Two to **three** servings a day to stay strong.

"Adventures in eating will now begin.
Come along with me, read this book I'm in.

Nutrition Champion of Kids, that's me.
Listening to what I say is the key.

Meet my food friends in the Food Pyramid.
Learn to eat healthy and smart as a kid.

To be sure you have fun, here's my one clue . . .
Never be afraid to try something new!"

Pyramid Pal

There is one more GROUP placed high at the top.
For FATS, OILS and SWEETS, before you eat, STOP!

"Empty Calories" are packed into all.
So, make sure your servings are always small.

Sal **Salad Dressing**, like a downpour, gushed.
Onto a salad, so quickly she rushed.

Oliver **Olive Oil** crooned his glad song.
"Come and join with me and please sing along.

If you use **Oil**, I am one of the best,
Scoring high in a heart healthy taste test."

Bart **Butter** and his friend Mark **Margarine**,
Knew they couldn't compare to **Oil** and win.

Stan **Sugar** sprinkled, quietly he fell,
Onto the cereal, he loved so well.

Courtney **Cupcake**, dressed in her paper skirt,
Knew that she was an elegant dessert.

Camilla **Cake** shouted out with great glee,
"For birthdays, no one is better than me."

Callie **Candy,** a sweet tightly wrapped treat,
With her sugary friends, strolled down the street.

Jealous Charles **Chocolate Bar** said, "I'm the best.
In every taste test, I beat all the rest."

Sara **Soft Drink**, screaming the word, "Diet",
Yelled, "No Sugar", and wouldn't keep quiet.

"I know lots of **Water** each day is best,
As necessary as food, play and rest."

Then, Chester **Chip** dropped and flopped from the shelf,
All crispy and salty, proud of himself.

Whether potato or corn, you can munch
Chips with a submarine sandwich for lunch.

Finally, Chad **Cookie**, proud, big and round,
Leaped from the jar where good munchies are found.

When it comes to nutrition, moms complain,
"There is little good that these foods contain."

For Fat and Calories, they are the worst.
Still, they do give a quick energy burst.

"Eat less, eat sparingly," words often said,
"And for your dessert, have fresh **FRUIT** instead."

Eating from this GROUP, please, do understand,
Tiny amounts are your very best plan.